Cobb-Cook School Library

AN EARLY CRAFT BOOK

AQUARIUMS

by PHIL STEINBERG pictures by GEORGE OVERLIE

Lerner Publications Company • Minneapolis, Minnesota

LIBRARY OF CONGRESS CATALOGING IN PUBLICATION DATA

Steinberg, Phillip.
  Aquariums.

  (An Early Craft Book)
  SUMMARY: Instructions for setting up and maintaining an aquarium with advice on selecting fishes and plants.

  1. Aquariums—Juvenile literature. [1. Aquariums] I. Overlie, George, ill. II. Title.

SF457.S67   639'.34   74-11889
ISBN 0-8225-0870-2

Copyright © 1975 by Lerner Publications Company

All rights reserved. International copyright secured. Manufactured in the United States of America. Published simultaneously in Canada by J. M. Dent & Sons (Canada) Ltd., Don Mills, Ontario.

International Standard Book Number: 0-8225-0870-2
Library of Congress Catalog Card Number: 74-11889

Contents

The underwater world 5
Fishes and oxygen 7
Clean water 9
Setting up an aquarium 10
Aquarium temperature 17
Planting the aquarium 18
All about fishes 21
Feeding your fishes 27
Keeping the aquarium clean 29
Keeping your fishes healthy 31
Things to remember 32

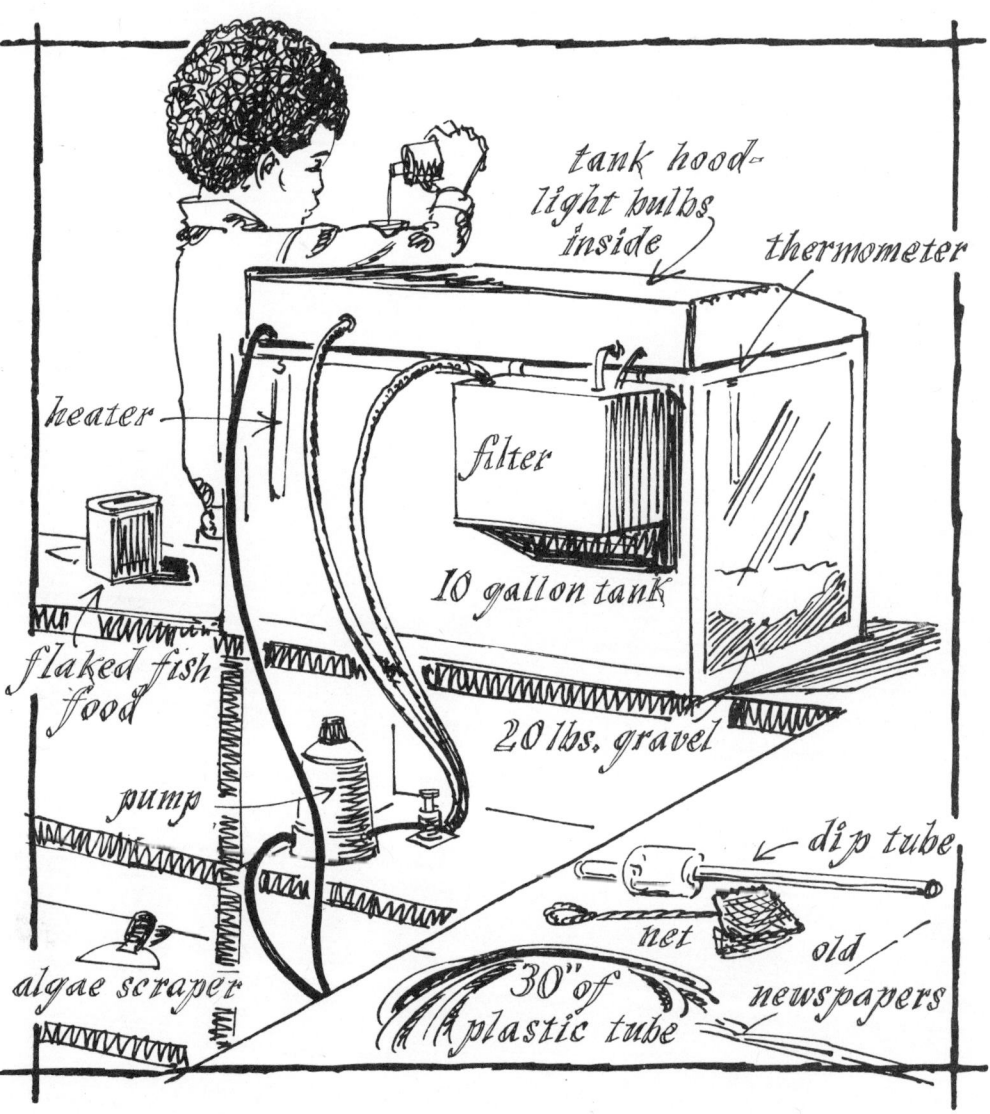

The underwater world

For thousands of years people have enjoyed keeping small brightly colored fishes. Many of the ancient Romans built shallow pools in their homes and filled them with colorful fishes for their guests to admire. For hundreds of years Japanese and Chinese people have raised fancy goldfish. Today many people still keep one or two goldfish and enjoy watching them swim in their round bowls. Out of this love for small colorful fishes has grown the hobby of keeping tropical fish in an aquarium.

Tropical fish are different from goldfish. Goldfish come from temperate, or mild, climates. But aquarium fish come from tropical climates—areas in which the weather is always warm. These fishes live in freshwater lakes, streams, and ponds in Central America, South America, Asia, and Africa. People who live there catch the fishes in large nets and ship

where tropical fish come from

angel fish

them to the United States and other places around the world. Some fishes are raised by tropical fish dealers in this country. You can buy both kinds of fishes in pet shops.

A tropical fish aquarium is much more than just a bowl of water with fishes in it. It is a hobby that has many responsibilities. The fishes cannot take care of themselves. They depend upon their owners for many things, such as a clean and comfortable place in which to live, friendly neighbors, and good food. When you set up a tropical fish aquarium, you are really creating a complete world for your fishes to live in. This world will have an underwater garden and it will be very much like a small tropical lake or pond.

If you set up your aquarium properly and take good care of it, you will be rewarded by having created a mysterious and fascinating underwater world. Your aquarium will have crystal-clear water, healthy green plants, and healthy, lively fishes.

Fishes and oxygen

In some ways fishes are like you and me. They need a clean place to live, proper food, and plenty of oxygen to breathe. Oxygen (OX-ih-jen) is a gas that both people and fishes must breathe in order to live.

Perhaps you have noticed that fishes open and close their mouths as though they are chewing. What they are really doing is breathing. They do this by drawing water into their mouths and passing it over tiny blood vessels in their cheeks called gills. Gills are covered by a thin plate of bone. But the gills themselves look like rows of red fringes. In some ways, fishes' gills are like our lungs. The gills take oxygen out of the water just as our lungs take oxygen out of the air.

If there is not enough oxygen in the water, the fishes will swim near the top of the tank and gulp for air. When they do this, something is wrong with the aquarium. The fishes are

7

plants help supply oxygen

choking. It can mean that there are too many fishes in the tank, or it can mean that there is something wrong with the water. This condition must be corrected right away, or the fishes will die.

The air that supplies oxygen to the water is absorbed, or taken on, at the surface of the tank. Most aquariums do not have enough surface area to supply all the oxygen the fishes need. There are two things you can do to increase the supply of oxygen. One of the things you can do is to be sure you have plenty of healthy plants growing in the tank. As fishes breathe, they use up oxygen and give off a harmful gas called carbon dioxide (KAR-bon die-OX-ide). Growing plants take on carbon dioxide and give off oxygen. Thus, plants not only use up harmful carbon dioxide, but they also produce oxygen fishes need.

Another thing that helps supply oxygen to the water is an aerator (AIR-rate-or). An aerator is a little electric machine that blows air into the water. There are two kinds you can buy. One is a motor-driven pump, and the other is a vibrator. The vibrator costs less and lasts longer. But they both do a good job. With both kinds, air is pumped through plastic tubes into an "air stone" on the bottom of the tank. The air stone is a special stone that gives off hundreds of tiny bubbles. These bubbles make the water move gently, and this gentle movement helps the water give up its carbon dioxide and absorb more oxygen.

Clean water

The pump or vibrator will operate another important piece of equipment—the filter. The filter keeps the water in your aquarium clean. There are several kinds of filters. One cleans the water by pumping it through a box that hangs outside the back of the tank. This box contains glass wool and charcoal. The wool and charcoal take the dirt out of the water. Then the cleaned water is pumped back into the tank.

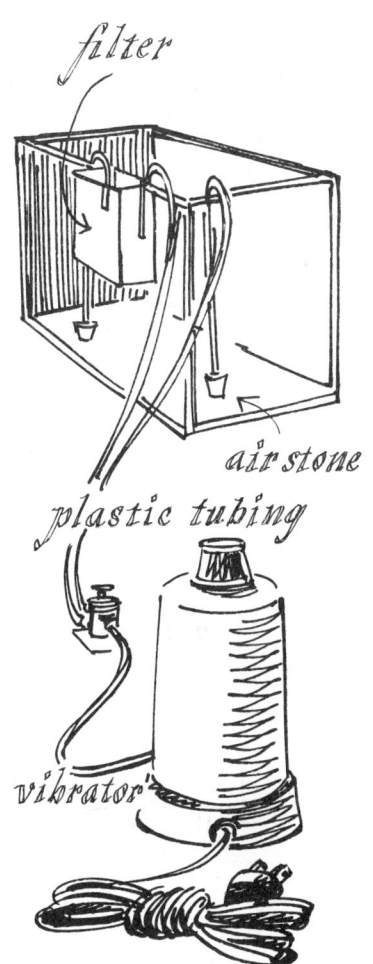

under-the-gravel filter

Another type of filter looks like a flat white pan. It is placed under the gravel in the tank. It cleans the water by filtering it through the gravel. I like this type because it does not take up much space, and it is out of sight. Some under-the-gravel filters use cartridges of charcoal that keep the water pure and remove bad odors. These cartridges do not cost very much. They are replaced once a month. With an under-the-gravel filter, you do not need an aerator, because the filter also produces bubbles that aerate the tank.

Setting up an aquarium

There are many things you must do to your aquarium before you can put in the fishes. It is important that you take your time and do everything the right way and in the proper order. If you do, you will be sure that your aquarium is set up correctly. Your fishes will be healthier and will live longer.

The first thing you must do is choose a fish tank. Tanks come in many sizes from one that holds two gallons (about eight liters) of water to one that holds 50 gallons (about 190 liters) of water. Which size should you get? I suggest you start with a 10-gallon (about 40-liters) tank. A 10-gallon tank, completely set up, will cost under $25. A smaller tank will cost almost as much. And, larger tanks are easier to keep in good condition. In larger tanks, the temperature of the water does not change too fast. The water stays clean longer. Plants thrive in a larger tank, and the fishes have more room in which to swim. If fishes are crowded in a small tank, they may not be friendly. And the most important reason for getting a 10-gallon tank instead of a smaller one is—it holds more fishes!

When you have chosen your tank and set up the aerator and filter, you must pick the place you wish to keep your aquarium. Picking the right spot is very important. Once a tank is set up it should not be moved because moving a full

tank can cause it to leak. Do not put your tank in front of a window. Daylight causes tiny green plants to grow on the aquarium glass. These plants are called algae (AL-jee). If you can prevent it, you do not want algae in your tank.

A good place for your aquarium is against a wall by an electrical outlet, and the best support for your tank is an aquarium stand. These stands are made of heavy metal. They come in all sizes to fit every tank. They cost about $15. If you do not wish to spend the money for an aquarium stand, be sure the table you use to hold your aquarium is strong and sturdy. Water weighs more than 8 pounds (about four kilograms) for each gallon. Therefore, a 10-gallon tank full of water will weigh more than 83 pounds (about 42 kilograms).

To keep your fishes and plants healthy, your aquarium should also have a lighted reflector. Electric light bulbs fit inside the reflector. These lights should be left on for 8 to 10 hours every day. A reflector covers just part of the top of the aquarium. You will need a thick sheet of glass to cover the other part. The glass will keep out dust and will keep the fishes from jumping out of the tank.

You can use an aquarium hood instead of a reflector. An aquarium hood covers the entire top of the tank and also has fixtures for electric light bulbs. A hood is better than a reflector, but it costs a little more.

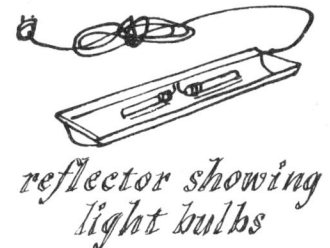
reflector showing light bulbs

hood with light bulbs

Whether you use a hood or reflector, it should be placed so that the light shines from the front of the aquarium to the back. Fishes look better in this kind of light. No light should come from behind the tank. This is one of the reasons many people paint the outside of the back of their aquariums.

To paint the back of your aquarium, you can use a special paint called "aquarium crystal paint." It comes in many colors. The most popular color is medium green. When this paint dries, it forms crystals that make interesting patterns on the glass. You can buy paint that

use water and salt to clean your aquarium

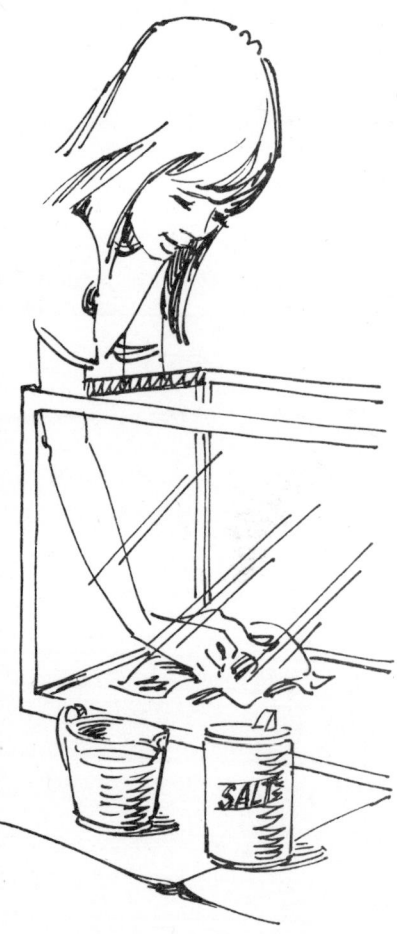

you use with a brush or you can buy spray-on paint. If you want to paint, you should do so before you put water in your aquarium. (If you wish to change the look of your aquarium, you can take the paint off by wetting it with soaked newspapers and by scraping.)

Another way to prevent light from entering at the back of your aquarium is to fit it with a mirror. This makes an interesting background, but it is more costly than paint.

Your tank should also be carefully cleaned before you put water into it. Do not use soap or glass cleaner on the inside of the tank. If any of the soap or cleaner is left in the tank it could harm your fishes. Water, table salt, and a dish towel will usually get the tank clean enough. When it is clean, rinsed, and dry, your tank is ready for the gravel.

Gravel is little pieces of rock made especially for aquariums. Most of your aquarium plants will be planted in the gravel. Gravel comes in many colors and sizes. The best size is a medium grade number two or three. Never use sand in your aquarium.

Many people like colored gravel because they think it adds beauty to their aquariums. I do not agree. Plain common gravel looks best in a well-planted aquarium. Colored gravel makes the water look colored, too, and it should be crystal clear.

How much gravel will you need? You will need enough gravel to cover the bottom of the tank to a depth of one and one-half inches in the front and two inches in the back. It takes two pounds (about one kilogram) of gravel for each gallon of water in your tank. A 10-gallon aquarium, therefore, needs 20 pounds (about 10 kilograms) of gravel.

The gravel must be washed before it is put into the tank. Put about five or six pounds of the gravel in a plastic pail and fill it with water. Stir the gravel with your hand or a wooden paddle. This loosens the dust and dirt. Pour out the dirty water. Fill the pail again and once

a 10-gallon aquarium needs 20 lbs. of gravel

cleaning gravel

place under-the-gravel filter on bottom – then start aerator

add gravel – stones and ornaments

fill slowly

newspaper

more stir up the gravel. Keep doing this until all the gravel is quite clean.

If you bought an under-the-gravel filter, place it on the bottom of the tank before you add the gravel. Spread out the gravel so it slopes from the back of the tank to the front of the tank. Now one or two interesting rocks may be placed on the gravel. There are other interesting ornaments you can put in your tank. Little ships, bridges, and caves add beauty to your aquarium. Buy the rocks and ornaments from a pet store. Be sure they are safe for your aquarium. Some rocks and all sea shells are not safe.

When the gravel and ornaments are in place, you can put water into your aquarium. Place a few sheets of newspaper on top of the gravel and slowly pour water into the tank until it is full. The newspapers keep the stream of water from digging holes in the gravel. Remove the newspapers carefully and get rid of them.

This next is the hardest part of setting up an aquarium. You must let the tank sit for four or five days before you plant your underwater garden and add the fishes. This waiting gives the water time to "age." The water we drink is treated with chemicals, such as chlorine, to make it safe for us to drink. But these chemicals will kill fishes. By letting the water sit for four or five days, the chemicals evaporate. Pet shops sell a liquid that removes the chlorine from the water, but aging the water is safer.

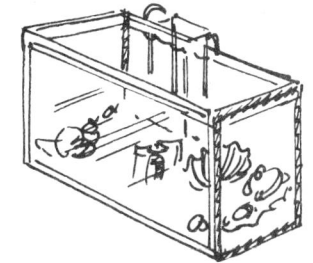
remove newspapers— then let water age for five days

Aquarium temperature

The temperature of the water is very important to the health of your fishes. The water should always be between 75 and 78 degrees Fahrenheit (about 24 to 26 degrees Celsius). To keep the water at this temperature, you will need an electric thermostat heater in your tank. It is one of the most important pieces of equipment in your aquarium. It has a little control knob on top. You set the temperature by turning this knob.

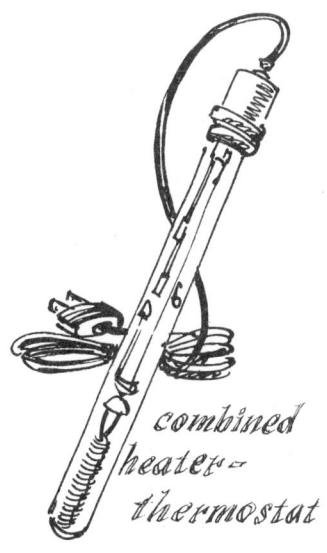
combined heater-thermostat

thermometer

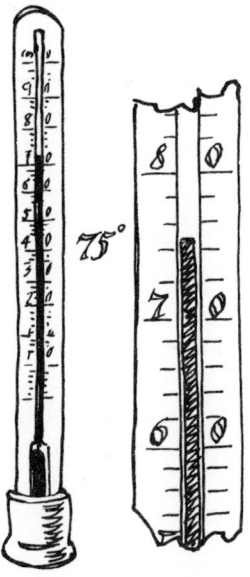

To be sure that the water is always at the right temperature, keep a thermometer in the tank. You can use a floating thermometer or one that hangs inside the tank. Look at the thermometer at least twice a day. If the water temperature is below 75 degrees, set the knob on the heater up. If the temperature is above 78 degrees, set the knob back a little. A sudden change in the temperature of the water will make your fishes sick. Remember that your fishes come from warm tropical climates. Never let the water temperature go below 75 degrees.

Planting the aquarium

Amazon sword plant

After the water has aged, you can plant your underwater garden. Some people plant their plants right away and then let the water age before adding their fishes. This is not the best way to plant. If there are no fishes in the tank, the plants may die. When the fishes eliminate wastes from their bodies, they add acid to the water. Plants grow best in water that has some acid in it. The plants also need the carbon dioxide the fishes give off.

Aquarium plants are divided into three groups, according to the way they are sold. The first group is made up of rooted plants. They must be planted in the gravel. The second group is made up of floating plants. The third group is made up of bunched plants. They are tied at the bottom with a lead weight or a rubber band.

You will want a few plants from each of these groups. Most of the rooted plants grow and produce new roots called runners. These runners, in turn, grow into new plants. One of the most popular of the rooted plants is the Amazon sword plant. You should have one of these beautiful plants as a center of interest in your underwater garden. Some other rooted plants are called ludwigia, eel grass, corkscrew, and sagittaria.

Duckweek and salvinia are two of the floating types of plants. These plants make good hiding

rooted plants

floating plants

bunched plants

rooted plant

planting with a forked stick

places for young and small fishes. But do not use too many floating plants. They will keep light from reaching the bottom of the tank. The bunched plants, among which are the ferny elodea and ambulia, can either hang in the water or be planted in the gravel.

The people at the pet shop will help you select the plants you like. All plants should be washed under the faucet before they are put into the aquarium. The tall plants, like eel grass and corkscrew, should be planted in the back of the aquarium. The shorter plants would look nice in front. Cover the roots of the rooted plants completely, but do not plant them too deep.

Two 20-inch sticks with notched ends are helpful when planting. Use one stick to hold the plant down and the other to cover the roots with gravel. If you have trouble planting in a full tank, remove a pail or two of water. After you have finished planting, lay newspapers on the water and gently fill the tank with the water you removed. Carefully take the newspapers out of the tank and make sure the temperature is right. Now, at last, your aquarium is ready for the fishes.

All about fishes

Guppy

There are two general types of tropical fishes. One type has babies that are hatched from eggs. These fishes are called egg-layers. The other type of tropical fish has babies that are born alive. These fishes are called live-bearers. All tropical fishes are either egg-layers or live-bearers.

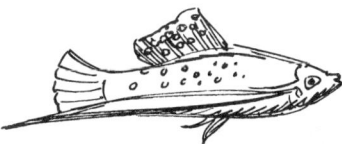
Swordtail (wild)

One of the most popular of all tropical fishes is the guppy. Male guppies have fancy tails and are brightly colored. When they grow up, they are about an inch long. The females are bigger than the males, but they are not as colorful.

Guppies are live-bearers. The eggs of guppies are kept inside the mother's body. The father guppy fertilizes the mother's eggs. When they are ready to swim, the babies are born. A

Black Molly

mother guppy will have from 6 to 60 babies at one time. She can have a new family every four to six weeks. The babies grow fast. In three or four months, they can have babies of their own. Guppies do not bother the other fishes in the tank, and they are easy to take care of.

The swordtail is another kind of live-bearer. The male swordtail is a strange-looking tropical fish because its tail looks like a long sword. Female swordtails do not have swords. These fishes are also friendly and will get along nicely with their neighbors.

Still another live-bearer is the black molly. It grows to about three inches in length. Its rich black color is a pleasing contrast to that of the light-colored fishes in your aquarium.

Platy (PLAT-ee) fishes, or moons, are also live-bearers. There are many different kinds of platys. They are friendly fishes, and they are nice to have in your aquarium.

Angel fishes are egg-layers. They are some of the most beautiful of the tropical fishes. The mother angel fish lays her eggs on the leaves of plants. The father fertilizes the eggs while they are on the leaves. After a time, the eggs hatch into baby angel fishes. Although angel fishes are very beautiful, they are not always friendly.

The neon tetra is a very small fish. Its red and blue colors are very bright, and it looks like a neon light. These beautiful fishes are fun to watch as they swim in groups, or schools. Neon tetras are also egg-layers. You might like about six or seven of them in your aquarium.

Another fish that swims in schools is the zebra fish. Its body is striped like a real zebra. The zebra fish will grow to about two inches in length. Zebra fishes are egg-layers, too. A school of about four or five zebra fishes will get along nicely with the other fish in your aquarium.

Tropical catfishes come from South America. Catfishes are scavengers. Scavengers eat things that many other fishes will not eat. Most tropical fishes will not eat the spoiled food that sinks to the bottom of the tank. Catfishes will

Zebra fish

Catfish

Hatchet fish

Glass fish

Clown Loach

Pencil fish

eat it. Thus, catfishes help keep the aquarium clean. It is fun to watch them dart about on the bottom of the aquarium. With their little whiskers they turn over every grain of gravel as they search for food. Because they help keep the tank clean, you should have one or two of them in your aquarium.

There are hundreds of different kinds of tropical fishes. Some are unusual because of their bright coloring, others because of their odd shapes. The hatchet fish is a fish that looks like a hatchet. The glass fish is so thin you can see through it. The clown loach looks as if he is dressed in a clown's costume. The pencil fish is long and thin like a pencil. Most pet shops sell these unusual fishes along with the common favorites.

It is always good to buy fishes in pairs, a male and a female, if you can. They are good company for each other. Many of the live-bearers, especially the guppies, will have babies in your tank. Do not be surprised if the bigger fishes eat some of these baby fishes. This is the way nature balances the fish population. If the big fishes did not eat most of the baby guppies, there would soon be hundreds of guppies in your tank. Then all your fishes would die because there would not be enough oxygen for them to breathe. If you want to raise the babies, you must put them in a separate tank.

How many fishes should you have in your aquarium? This is a hard question to answer. There is no set rule that we can depend upon. If your 10-gallon aquarium is well planted and aerated, it can safely hold 20 to 25 small fishes. Do not overstock your aquarium. Fishes stay healthier and grow better if they are not crowded. If your fishes stay at the top of the tank, you may have too many fishes in your aquarium. It is better to have too few fishes than too many.

Tropical fishes are usually brought home from the pet shop in a plastic bag or a waxed paper cup. Float these containers in your tank

balancing the aquarium population

this aquarium has too many fish

fish at the top

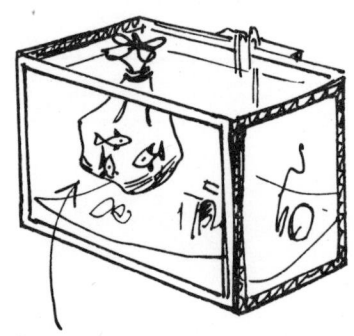

container of new fish – float in tank for 45 minutes

snails help keep the aquarium clean

for at least 45 minutes before you open them and set the fishes free. This will let the temperature in the containers slowly change to the temperature of the water in your aquarium. Any sudden change in temperature is bad for the fishes.

Should you have snails in your tank? Snails are fun to watch and add interest to your aquarium. They will help keep your aquarium clean by eating algae and spoiled food. Some snails have so many babies that the tank gets too full of snails. You do not want this kind of snail. They will eat your plants. A good snail to have in your aquarium is the apple or mystery snail. It grows to be about the size of a small walnut. This snail lays its eggs out of water, usually on the inside of the hood of the tank. By removing these eggs, you can control the number of snails in your aquarium.

The mystery snail must breathe air. Therefore, once in a while, you will see it climb to the top of the tank. It will stick something out of its shell that looks like a funnel. Then it will pump its body until it has taken in all the air it needs, and it will sink to the bottom of the tank. Sometimes it will lie on the bottom of the tank and not move for hours. Watch it closely. It if does not move after one day, it may be dead. Dead snails make the water smell bad. They should be removed from the tank.

Feeding your fishes

There are three kinds of food you can feed your fishes. One is a dry food that comes in small boxes or cans. It is called "flaked" food and is the most popular of all fish foods. You should sprinkle a pinch of flaked food on the top of the water.

The second kind of fish food is frozen and must be kept in the freezer compartment of your refrigerator. This food is made up of small shrimp and sea scallops. You can chop a piece of this food off the larger piece with a knife. Then put it in a fish net and hold it under the

thaw frozen fish food under a faucet

feed a little bit **3** *times a day*

DO NOT OVERFEED!

give them only as much food as they can eat in about 2 minutes

faucet until it thaws. When is is thawed, drop it on the surface of the water.

The third kind of food is live fish food. The most popular live foods are white worms, brine shrimp, or cut-up earthworms.

For the most part, you can feed your fishes the flaked fish food. But about once a month, you can treat them to a meal of frozen or live food. Do not feed the fishes the first day you get them. Let them get used to the aquarium, for if they are excited, they will not eat and the food will spoil. Give the fishes only as much food as they can eat in about two minutes. Food that is not eaten will sink to the bottom of the tank and may eventually pollute the water if it is not eaten by your scavengers or cleaned out of the tank.

It is better to feed your fishes a little bit of food three times a day than to give them a lot of food just once a day. Do not overfeed them. Remember, too, that fishes will not eat in the dark, so do not put out the aquarium lights too soon after feeding.

Keeping the aquarium clean

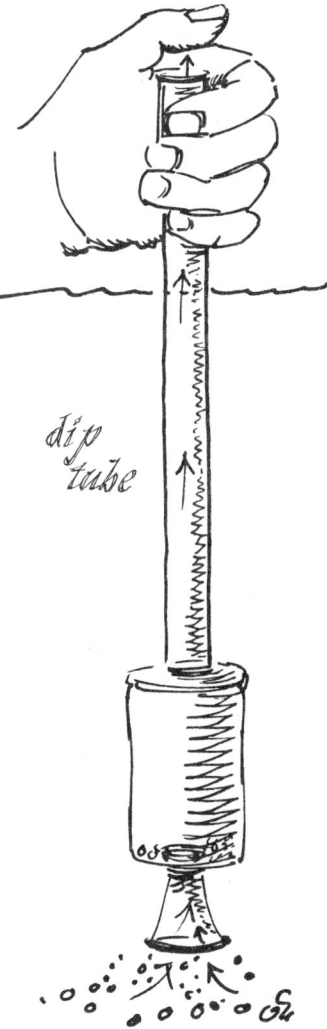

A properly set up aquarium will have crystal-clear water, healthy plants, and lively fishes. In order for the aquarium to stay this way, it must be cleaned at least once a month. The best way to clean an aquarium is to use a dip tube. A dip tube is a plastic tube about 18 inches long. It has a big plastic bubble near the bottom. To make it work, hold your finger over the top of the tube. Stick the tube into the water until it almost touches the gravel. Take your finger away from the top of the tube. Like magic, the bubble will fill up with water. This water will carry with it the dirt that is hidden in the gravel. Now put your finger back over the top of the tube and remove the tube from the tank. Empty the dip tube into a waste container. Repeat this process several times until you have covered most of the bottom of the tank.

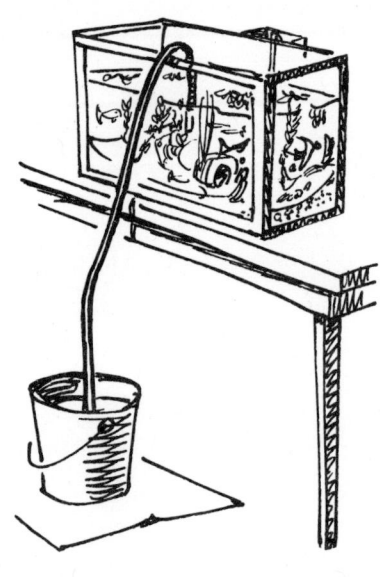

once a month siphon off 1/3 of the water — refill with aged water

Also, once a month, a third of the water in the tank should be replaced. Use a rubber tube as a siphon. Move one end of the tube around close to the bottom of the tank and the water will drain out of the other end of the tube. Be sure to have that end hanging in a pail. When you have removed enough water, carefully add more aged water to refill the tank. It is wise to always have a plastic pail full of water sitting some place out of sight. If you do, you will always have aged water when you need it. If you use a siphon near the first of each month and a dip tube near the middle of each month, your aquarium will stay as clean as it should be. Never replace more than a third of the water at one time. Too much fresh water might make your fishes sick.

You must keep your aquarium free of algae, too. Even though direct sunlight may not reach your aquarium, some algae can form on the inside of the glass. This should be removed with an algae scraper. An algae scraper is a blade on a long handle. You can also use a fine grade of steel wool for cleaning the glass, or you can use an aquarium sponge. Any of these items can be bought at a pet shop.

Once a year your aquarium should be completely drained and cleaned. Put your fishes and plants in plastic pails with the water you drain out of the tank. Remove the gravel and clean it or replace it with new washed gravel. Clean the filters and set up your aquarium as you did the first time.

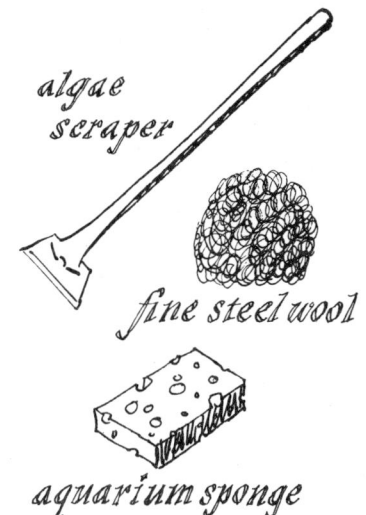

Keeping your fish healthy

Most tropical fishes live for about two or three years. Some of them, like the glass fish and the hatchet fish, live only about six months. But tropical fishes can get sick. The most common illness is called "ich" (IK) or "white spot disease." If your fishes get this illness, white spots will appear on their bodies. The disease can spread to all the fishes in your tank.

Your pet shop has medicine you can put in your tank to cure the fishes. Keeping the water at 80 degrees for a week may also help your fishes to get well.

Things to remember

Set up your aquarium carefully.

Always use aged water.

Don't keep too many fishes in your aquarium.

Don't overfeed your fishes.

Don't let the water temperature get get below 75 degrees.

Keep your aquarium clean.

If you remember and do all these things, your aquarium will be a thing of beauty that you will enjoy for a very long time.